THE
2007
GRIFFIN
POETRY
PRIZE
ANTHOLOGY

The 2007 Griffin Poetry Prize Anthology

A SELECTION OF THE SHORTLIST

Edited by KAREN SOLIE

ANANSI

Published in 2007 by
House of Anansi Press Inc.
110 Spadina Avenue, Suite 801
Toronto, ON, M5V 2K4
Tel. 416-363-4343
Fax 416-363-1017
www.anansi.ca

Distributed in Canada by
HarperCollins Canada Ltd.
1995 Markham Road
Scarborough, ON, M1B 5M8
Toll free tel. 1-800-387-0117

Distributed in the United States by
Publishers Group West
1700 Fourth Street
Berkeley, CA 94710
Toll free tel. 1-800-788-3123

The Griffin Trust and "POETRY" logos used with permission.
Pages 92–93 constitute a continuation of this copyright page.

11 10 09 08 07   1 2 3 4 5

Library and Archives Canada Cataloguing in Publication Data

The 2007 Griffin poetry prize anthology : a selection of the shortlist / Karen Solie, editor.
ISBN-13: 978-0-88784-764-6 · ISBN-10: 0-88784-764-1
1. English poetry — 21st century. 2. Canadian poetry (English) — 21st century.
I. Solie, Karen, 1966– II. Title: Two thousand and seven Griffin poetry prize anthology.
PS8293.1.T96 2007   821'.9208   C2007-900468-7

Library of Congress Control Number: 2007921133

Cover design: Scott Thornley + Company Inc.
Cover art: Sylvia Safdie
Text design and layout: Ingrid Paulson

Canada Council   Conseil des Arts
for the Arts   du Canada

ONTARIO ARTS COUNCIL
CONSEIL DES ARTS DE L'ONTARIO

*We acknowledge for their financial support of our publishing program
the Canada Council for the Arts, the Ontario Arts Council, and the Government of Canada
through the Book Publishing Industry Development Program (BPIDP).*

Printed and bound in Canada

CONTENTS

CANADIAN FINALISTS

PREFACE

EVERY NOW AND THEN, an essay, panel, blog, or lecture will be devised around the question, Is poetry dead? It's not that this question mustn't be asked. But I'd say the answer is no. As I watched the courier carry nine boxes of poetry — nearly 500 books — to my front door, it was a thrilled, vertiginous, slightly panicky no. Though, of course, numbers are not the point here. What is important is that the writer's vocation to attend to the world and to the ways we think about it, how we act in and upon it, continues to inspire challenging and innovative poetry of diverse content, form, technique, and tone. As it always has. In adjudicating the 2007 Griffin Poetry Prize, John Burnside, Charles Simic, and I were afforded the rare opportunity to appreciate individual collections within the context of most of the poetry published in English last year. As bodies of work go, it's healthy.

Inquiries into the well-being of poetry often have at least as much to do with whether anyone is reading it as with the quantity and sort of writing produced. Poetry is not a mainstream commodity; but commodity value is not the only value, and to exist outside the mainstream is not death. It does not even constitute a failure to thrive. For poetry's readership does thrive — again, as it always has — and does so in a way not necessarily indicated by Amazon rankings. As a reader, I know that poetry engages the heart and mind in a way that simply makes life better. More complicated. More interesting. Good poetry, like all good art, has changed people's lives. It has saved people's lives. There are readers among you who know this, and readers among you who will find out.

I encountered many very good books during two months of reading toward the Griffin Prize shortlist, including a number of happy surprises both from writers whose work I knew and from those I hadn't read before. Because it became more and more difficult to narrow the field, I found quite remarkable how many selections John, Charles, and I had in common when it came time for our first phone conversation. The shortlist, however, was hardly a foregone conclusion. Cases made, questions asked, and requests for rereads satisfied, we arrived at a decision that we believe fulfills the prize's mandate to recognize excellence in the field.

Good poetry demonstrates a commitment and responsibility to ideas, to beauty, and to craft that can throw a wrench into habits of thinking and perception. Good poetry can open our eyes a little. It can make things new. To acknowledge the value of poetry is to acknowledge the human imperative to pay attention. And we see every day what happens when people don't pay attention.

For the reader, alone in the peculiar way one is alone with a book, poetry can generate a simultaneously visceral and intellectual charge that is singular and addictive. In my memory the early months of 2007 will remain conspicuous for the amount of time I sat with a book of poems in my hands, feeling like the top of my head was about to come off, as my first Maritime winter piled up outside. For this I thank both the poets on the shortlist and those who are not. It is a primary function of anthologies to introduce readers to writers they may not yet have encountered, and for those of you who are new to any or all of the work represented here, I envy you in the way readers envy each other the beginning of a good read. Have fun. There's more where this came from.

Karen Solie
Fredericton, NB, April 2007

INTERNATIONAL
FINALISTS

PAUL FARLEY

Tramp in Flames

Paul Farley is a poet of wit, sensuality, and warmth. His work engages with the commonplace and the overlooked, the absurd, and the catastrophic, the scientific and the mythic, in ways that make us stop and think again about what it is to be living in this particular world, at this particular moment in our history. Though he wears his learning lightly, Farley draws upon philosophy and natural science, as well as a deep, occasionally elegiac affection for the streets and fields and hillsides of the places he has called home, to create a poetry of exceptional formal skill. What makes his work so remarkable is that, whatever his subject matter, from the city of Liverpool to an old Ovaltine tin, everything is transformed by his imagination and his formal gifts, making us think again about what we know, and what we think we know. That said, however, what comes across most vividly here is the sheer music of the writing: every line sings off the page, and there can be few poets whose work is so memorable. If the best poetry aspires to the condition of music, as Mallarmé suggests, then this is poetry of the highest order: melodic, humane, and intellectually engaging, *Tramp in Flames* renews our contract with the given world, yet challenges us to think again about what we see, and what we take for granted.

The Lapse

When the cutting edge was a sleight, a trick of time,
we blinked our way through *Jason and the Argonauts*,
thrilled by the stop-motion universe,
its brazen Talos grinding like a Dock Road crane,
and the Hydra's teeth sown into studio soil
by Harryhausen, who got between the frames
like a man who comes in bone dry from a downpour
by stopping the world and snapping out a path
through glassy rods right up to his front door.

Something as simple as Edgerton's milk splash
stilled to an ivory coronet would do it,
keep us quiet for hours as we learned to understand
the howling gale we stood in. Chilled to the core
we gasped as Ursula Andress stepped from the flame
and the unseen British-Pathé make-up department
took down her face, applying gravity with a trowel.
And I'd have to say something was taken from us.

On the dead sheep's seconds-long journey to nothing
with maggots working like a ball of fire,
every now and then a long bone settled awkwardly
like a break in continuity. Like an afternoon
of finding out for ourselves what death smelt like.
Long afternoons. Lying on our backs watching clouds
with the slow Doppler of a plane being bowed across the sky.
Give us back the giant day. Give us back what's ours.

Liverpool Disappears for a Billionth of a Second

Shorter than the blink inside a blink
the National Grid will sometimes make, when you'll
turn to a room and say: *Was that just me?*

People sitting down for dinner don't feel
their chairs taken away/put back again
much faster than that trick with tablecloths.

A train entering the Olive Mount cutting
shudders, but not a single passenger
complains when it pulls in almost on time.

The birds feel it, though, and if you see
starlings in shoal, seagulls abandoning
cathedral ledges, or a mob of pigeons

lifting from a square as at gunfire,
be warned, it may be happening, but then
those sensitive to bat-squeak in the backs

of necks, who claim to hear the distant roar
of comets on the turn — these may well smile
at a world restored, in one piece; though each place

where mineral Liverpool goes wouldn't believe
what hit it: all that sandstone out to sea
or meshed into the quarters of Cologne.

I've felt it a few times when I've gone home,
if anything, more often now I'm old,
and the gaps between get shorter all the time.

The Newsagent

My clock has gone although the sun has yet to take the sky.
I thought I was the first to see the snow, but his old eyes
have marked it all before I catch him in his column of light:
a rolled up metal shutter-blind, a paper bale held tight

between his knees so he can bring his blade up through the twine,
and through his little sacrifice he frees the day's headlines:
its strikes and wars, the weather's big seize up, runs on the pound.
One final star still burns above my head without a sound

as I set off. The dark country I grew up in has gone.
Ten thousand unseen dawns will settle softly on this one.
But with the streets all hushed I take the papers on my round
into the gathering blue, wearing my luminous armband.

Brutalist

Try living in one. Hang washing out to dry
and break its clean lines with your duds and smalls.
Spray tribal names across its subway walls
and crack its flagstones so the weeds can try

their damnedest. That's the way. Fly-tip the lives
you led, out past its edge, on the back field;
sideboards and mangles made sense in the peeled
spud light of the old house but the knives

are out for them now. This cellarless, unatticked
place will shake the rentman off, will throw
open its arms and welcome the White Arrow
delivery fleet which brings the things on tick

from the slush piles of the seasonal catalogues.
The quilt boxes will take up residence
on the tops of white wardrobes, an ambulance
raise blinds, a whole geography of dogs

will make their presence felt. And once a year
on Le Corbusier's birthday, the sun will set
bang on the pre-ordained exact spot
and that is why we put that slab just there.

One by one the shopkeepers will shut
their doors for good. A newsagent will draw
the line at buttered steps. The final straw
will fill the fields beyond. Now live in it.

Tramp in Flames

Some similes act like heat shields for re-entry
to reality: a tramp in flames on the floor.
We can say *Flame on!* to invoke the Human Torch
from the Fantastic Four. We can switch to art
and imagine Dali at this latitude
doing CCTV surrealism.
We could compare him to a protest monk
sat up the way he is. We could force the lock
of memory: at the crematorium
my uncle said the burning bodies rose
like Draculas from their boxes.
                                        But his layers
burn brightly, and the salts locked in his hems
give off the colours of a Roman candle,
and the smell is like a foot-and-mouth pyre
in the middle of the city he was born in,
and the bin bags melt and fuse him to the pavement
and a pool forms like the way he wet himself
sat on the school floor forty years before,
and then the hand goes up. *The hand goes up.*

An Ovaltine Tin in the Egg Collections at Tring

If, at the end of the day as they say, these eggs
tell a story set in negative space, then it's right
the tin I caught sight of stacked in a corner
should have its say, a battered by-product
brought in after a spring-clean or a clear-out;
I could play it over my knee, bash out a tune,
but prefer to let this one speak for itself,
emptied twice over, if you see what I mean,

shiny inside, metallic as the moon,
the outside meant for a world I don't understand
just as a blackbird's egg seems out of place
laid out on cotton wool, removed from leaf shadow
or nettle bed. Caskets for collections
of garden birds, I say speak for yourselves
and there's just a huge silence of course, although
the brand names call out, as they were designed to:

Craven A, Huntley & Palmers, Oxo,
Crawford's, Jacob's, Peak Frean's Assorted Creams,
Selesta Fondants, Ogden's, Ovaltine...
Some sing on while others ring hollow,
a half-remembered jingle from the undergrowth
that turns this tin into a kind of music box,
and when I push and seal the lid back on
there's a silence twice over, if you see what I mean.

"A Shepherd's Guide to Wool and Earmarks"

Did Moses Mossop sit above Bowmanstead
with a book in early nineteenth-century rain?
He could have done: a drop has smudged his entry
in this knackered *Shepherd's Guide*, where Herdwicks graze

identically on every recto page
but for a second running through the press
that added the earmarks, and so identified
each flock to owner, and kept things up-to-date;

and sheltering by a sheepfold's leeward wall
he might have studied this on afternoons
of deepening lows, with fine drizzle broadcast
across each chapter — Seascale to Subberthwaite —

admiring these perfect, printed sheep,
his mind breeding a May of perfect lambs;
or thumbed its pages quickly so the ears
flickered to life and leapt like inky flames,

and with such animations passed his hours
as mine do, marooned in this dark hostel
with its puzzles and whodunits, all the paths
taped off and bleached, the scene of some huge crime.

The Scarecrow Wears a Wire

The scarecrow wears a wire in the top field.
At sundown, the audiophilic farmer
who bugged his pasture unpicks the concealed
mics from its lapels. He's by the fire

later, listening back to the great day,
though to the untrained ear there's nothing much
doing: a booming breeze, a wasp or bee
trying its empty button-hole, a stitch

of wrensong now and then. But he listens late
and nods off to the creak of the spinal pole
and the rumble of his tractor pulling beets
in the bottom field, which cuts out. In a while

somebody will approach over ploughed earth
in caked Frankenstein boots. There'll be a noise
of tearing, and he'll flap awake by a hearth
grown cold, waking the house with broken cries.

Paperboy and Air Rifle

A little hunter, I could have shouldered a gun
in the Highlands or Apennines. I would have loved
a wax jacket with a poacher's pocket sewn in,
but at Gerrard's Lane, where I reached the furthest point

and letterbox from the newsagent, where the fields
began, I took wood micks, shebbies, spadgers;
would have taken game if there'd been any to take;
would have knocked a partridge from the head of her brood,

I was that mean. I was doing all right at school,
shining in English composition, my similes
like my reading age running on ahead of the class:
The instant noodles hang from the end of my fork

like a Portuguese man-o-war. But I lived for the light nights
walking home on my own, all the papers delivered, a bird
in the bag. I've never been happier than the time
I got a goldfinch, looked it over in my hand —

just a line of blood between the mandibles —
and, taking the shortcut through a thistle field,
a summer's worth of goldfinches, the rest of his charm,
flew with me, a little ahead of me, from crown to crown.

The Westbourne at Sloane Square

You again! Of all the bomb-scarred stonework
and air vents underfoot I knew by heart.
You, still going strong in your black pipe
above the passengers and mice-live tracks.
You, flowing through eighteenth-century parkscape
into an ironclad late-Victorian night.

Pissed and standing on the eastbound platform
I was a tin soldier who'd fallen in
to London's storm drain, sent spinning around
the Circle Line long after closing time,
and all along I've carried these trapped sounds
I hear again and recognise deep down.

How many miles of shit have you crawled through
since we last met? I'd do it all again.
We've less choice than we think, the likes of you and me.
Blind water, borne along or bearing through,
escaping in a hurry for open sea.
To think we start as innocent as rain.

RODNEY JONES

Salvation Blues

There are not many poets who get as much of American
life in their poems as Rodney Jones. His *Salvation Blues*,
a book made up of one hundred poems taken from six
previous collections published over the last twenty
years, brings to mind Whitman. Jones asks in a poem,
What happened to all the people the older poet cheered
westward across the continent? They are all here in his
poems, making ends meet, working as farmers, shipping
clerks, waitresses, car mechanics, butchers, strippers,
and teachers, while trying their best to believe in the
American dream and a religion whose preachers tend
to be actors and salesmen whose pulpit is television.
Jones is a marvellous storyteller and a contemplative
man with an interest in both character and the way the
world works. "Most of us are compositions that begin in
error," he says. He never forgets that. His poems are
angry, bawdy, funny, wise, and deeply moving. They sing
to remind us of our humanity and to heal the language
of its long service as a mere tool.

I Find Joy in the Cemetery Trees

I find joy in the cemetery trees.
Their roots are in our hearts.
In their leaves the soul
of another century is in ascension.
I hear the rustling of their branches
and watch the exhausted laborers
from the Burgreen Construction Company
sit down in the shade,
unwrapping their ham and salami
and popping open their thermoses.
Apparently, they too are enamored
of the hickory and willow
at the edge of our cemetery.
They are stretching twine, building a wall
as though this could be contained.
Probably they do not think
of our grandmothers who are pierced,
and probably they do not want
to hear about Thomas Hardy,
who, if I remember, has been dead
longer than they have been alive,
and who gave to the leaves of one yew
the names of his own dead. Anyway
the only spirits I can call in this place
are the stench of a possum
suppurating in secret weeds
and the flies, who are marvelous
because their appetite is our revulsion.
Let the laborers go on. Right now
I wish I could admire the trees simply

for their architecture. All winter
the dying have set their tables
and now they are almost as black
as the profound waters off Guam.
A few minutes ago, when they started
in a slight breeze off the lake,
the many and patient sails,
I could see in those motions
a little of the world that owns me —
and that I cannot understand —
rise in its indifferent passion.

The Work of Poets

Willie Cooper, what are you doing here, this early in your death?

To show us what we are, who live by twisting words—
Heaven is finished. A poet is as anachronistic as a blacksmith.

You planted a long row and followed it. Signed your name X for
  seventy years.
Poverty is not hell. Fingers cracked by frost
And lacerated by Johnson grass are not hell.

Hell is what others think we are.

You told me once, "Never worry."
Your share of worry was as small as your share of the profits,

Mornings-after of lightning and radiator shine,
The beater Dodge you bought in late October—
By February, its engine would hang from a rafter like a ham.

You had a free place to stay, a wife
Who bore you fourteen children. Nine live still.

You live in the stripped skeleton of a shovelbill cat.

Up here in the unforgivable amnesia of libraries,
Where many poems lie dying of first-person omniscience,
The footnotes are doing their effete dance, as always.

But only one of your grandsons will sleep tonight in Kilby Prison.
The hackberry in the sand field will be there long objectifying.

Once I was embarrassed to have to read for you
A letter from Shields, your brother in Detroit,
A hick-grammared, epic lie of northern women and money.

All I want is to get one grain of the dust to remember.

I think it was your advice I followed across the oceans.
What can I do for you now?

TV

All the preachers claimed it was Satan.
Now the first sets seem more venerable
Than Abraham or Williamsburg
Or the avant-garde. Back then nothing,

Not even the bomb, had ever looked so new.
It seemed almost heretical watching it
When we visited relatives in the city,
Secretly delighting, but saying later,

After church, probably it would not last,
It would destroy things: standards
And the sacredness of words in books.
It was well into the age of color,

Korea and Little Rock long past,
Before anyone got one. Suddenly some
Of them in the next valley had one.
You would know them by their lights

Burning late at night, and the recentness
And distance of events entering their talk,
But not one in our valley; for a long time
No one had one, so when the first one

Arrived in the van from the furniture store
And the men had set the box on the lawn,
At first we stood back from it, circling it
As they raised its antenna and staked in

The guy wires before taking it in the door,
And I seem to recall a kind of blue light
Flickering from inside and then a woman
Calling out that they had got it tuned in —

A little fuzzy, a ghost picture, but something
That would stay with us, the way we hurried
Down the dirt road, the stars, the silence,
Then everyone disappearing into the houses.

The Assault on the Fields

It was like snow, if snow could blend with air and hover,
     making, at first,
A rolling boil, mottling the pine thickets behind the fields,
     but then flattening
As it spread above the fenceposts and the whiteface cattle,
     an enormous, luminous tablet,

A shimmering, an efflorescence, through which my father
     rode on his tractor,
Masked like a Martian or a god to create the cloud where
     he kept vanishing;
Though, of course, it was not a cloud or snow, but poison,
     dichlorodiphenyltrichloroethane,

The word like a bramble of black locust on the tongue,
     and, after a while,
It would fill the entire valley, as, one night in spring,
     five years earlier,
A man from Joe Wheeler Electric had touched a switch
     and our houses filled with light.

Already some of the music from the radio went with me
     when the radio was off.
The bass, the kiss of the snare. Some of the thereness
     rubbing off on the hereness.
But home place still meant family. Misfortune was a well
     of yellowish sulfur water.

The Flowerses lived next door. Coyd drove a road grader
        for the county.
Martha baked, sewed, or cleaned, complaining beautifully
        of the dust
Covering her new Formica counters. Martha and Coyd,
        Coyd Jr., Linda, and Jenny.

How were they different from us? They owned a television,
Knew by heart each of the couples on Dick Clark's
        American Bandstand.
At dusk Junior, the terrible, would beat on a cracked
        and unfrettable Silvertone guitar

While he pitched from the top of his wayward voice
        one of a dozen songs
He'd written for petulant freshman girls. "Little Patti,"
        "Matilda,"
"Sweet Bonnie G." What did the white dust have to do with anything?

For Junior, that year, it was rock 'n' roll; if not rock 'n' roll,
        then abstract expressionism —
One painting comes back. Black frame. Black canvas —
        "I call it *Death,*" he would say,
Then stomp out onto the front lawn to shoot his .22 rifle
        straight into the sky above his head.

Surely if Joel Shapiro's installation of barbed wire and
        crumbled concrete blocks,
In a side room of the most coveted space in Manhattan,
        pays homage

To the most coveted space in Manhattan, then Junior
    Flowers's *Death*,
Hanging on a wall dingy with soot in North Alabama,
    is a comment, too.

Are they the same thing? I do not know that they are not
    the same thing.
And the white dust, so magical, so poisonous: how does it
    differ from snow?
As it thins gradually over many nights, we don't notice
    it; once the golden

Carp have rotted from the surfaces of ponds, there is no
    stench to it;
It is more of an absence of things barely apprehended,
    of flies, of moths;
Until one day the hawks who patrolled the air over the chicken coops
    are gone;

And when a woman, who was a girl then, finds a lump,
    what does it have to do
With the green fields and the white dust boiling
    and hovering?
When I think of the name Jenny Flowers, it is that
    whiteness I think of.

Some bits have fallen to clump against a sheet of tin roofing
The tornado left folded in the ditch, and she stoops there
    to gather
A handful of chalk to mark the grounds for hopscotch.

Sitting with Others

The front seats filled last. Laggards, buffoons,
and kiss-ups falling in beside local politicos,
the about to be honored, and the hard of hearing.

No help from the middle, blenders and criminals.
And the back rows: restless, intelligent, unable to commit.
My place was always left-center, a little to the rear.

The shy sat with me, fearful of discovery.
Behind me the dead man's illegitimate children
and the bride's and groom's former lovers.

There, when lights were lowered, hands
plunged under skirts or deftly unzipped flies,
and, lights up again, rose and pattered in applause.

Ahead, the bored practiced impeccable signatures.
But was it a movie or a singing? I remember
the whole crowd uplifted, but not the event

or the word that brought us together as one —
One, I say now, when I had felt myself many,
speaking and listening: that was the contradiction.

FREDERICK SEIDEL

Ooga-Booga

Frederick Seidel's work reminds us that it is not poetry's job to reassure, to confirm expectations and habits of thought. Its beauty is often difficult and its pleasures complicated and unnerving. Violent, scary, uncomfortably funny, ferociously sad, angry, or in love, the poems' brutal honesty of intellect and instinct is written with wicked, magnificent control. And always, they are utterly human. Morality is never excused from the mess of politics and culture. "Civilized is about having stuff," writes Seidel. "Too much is almost enough." Addressing privilege and complicity in the first person, the poems know that for all that is acquired, somebody, or something, pays. "The American trophies covered in tears that deck the American halls" dog the boutique hotels, shadowing corners of those poems in which "We lived like hummingbirds on nectar and oxygen." *Ooga-Booga* places in uneasy proximity images and statements that, in the discomfort of the other's glare, reveal their underpinnings and implications. Its poems refuse complacency and the inertia of despair, whether from trajectories of loss, war, movies, hunting, cocktails at the Carlyle, or superbike racing. It bids us take a look at our own affairs. Seidel has written a startling, haunting book. Its risks are both its challenge and reward.

From Nijinsky's Diary

And when the doctor told me that I could have died.
And when I climbed up from the subway to the day outside.
White summer clouds were boiling in the trees.
I felt like falling to my knees.
Stand clear of the closing doors, please! Stand clear of the closing doors, please!

And when the camel knelt to let me mount it.
Winged angels knelt in silhouette
To worship at the altar made of blue
That the sun was fastened to.
It all came down to you. It all comes down to you.

In New York City "kneeling" buses kneel for the disabled.
My camel kneels. We fly into the desert.
I flee in terror to my tranquilizer the Sahara.
I stroll slowly down sweet Broadway.
It is as you say. We are here to pray.

On Being Debonair

Shirts wear themselves out being worn.
Suits fit perfectly,
But a man does
Decades of push-ups and no longer fits.
I take myself out to dinner.
It is a joy to sit alone
Without a book.
I use myself up being fine while I dine.
I am a result of the concierge at the Carlyle.
I order a bottle of Bordeaux.
I am a boulevard of elegance
In my well-known restaurants.

The moon comes over to my table.
Everything about her is typical.
I like the way she speaks to me.
Everything about me is bespoke.
You are not
Known, and you are not no one.
I remember you from before.
Sometimes I don't go out till the end of the day.
I simply forget till
I rush out, afraid the day will end.
Every sidewalk tree is desperate
For someone.

The desert at this time of year
Is troops in desert camouflage.
Bring in the unmanned drones.
I dine with my Carlyle smile.
She tells me spring will come.
The moon stops by my table
To tell me.
I will cut your heart out
And drink the rubies and eat the coral.
I like the female for its coral.
I go to Carnegie Hall
To make her open her mouth onstage and scream.

Homage to Pessoa

I once loved,
I thought I would be loved,
But I wasn't loved.
I wasn't loved for the only reason that matters —
It was not to be.
I unbuttoned my white gloves and stripped each off.
I set aside my gold-knobbed cane.
I picked up this pen...
And thought how many other men
Had smelled the rose in the bud vase
And lifted a fountain pen,
And lifted a mountain...
And put the shotgun in their mouth,
And noticed that their hunting dog was pointing.

Fog

I spend most of my time not dying.
That's what living is for.
I climb on a motorcycle.
I climb on a cloud and rain.
I climb on a woman I love.
I repeat my themes.

Here I am in Bologna again.
Here I go again.
Here I go again, getting happier and happier.
I climb on a log
Torpedoing toward the falls.
Basically, it sticks out of me.

At the factory,
The racer being made for me
Is not ready, but is getting deadly.
I am here to see it being born.
It is snowing in Milan, the TV says.
They close one airport, then both.

The Lord is my shepherd and the Director of Superbike Racing.
He buzzes me through three layers of security
To the innermost secret sanctum of the racing department
Where I will breathe my last.
Trains are delayed.
The Florence sky is falling snow.

Tonight Bologna is fog.
This afternoon, there it was,
With all the mechanics who are making it around it.
It stood on a sort of altar.
I stood in a sort of fog,
Taking digital photographs of my death.

The Owl You Heard

The owl you heard hooting
In the middle of the night wasn't me.
It was an owl.
Or maybe you were
So asleep you didn't even hear it.
The sprinklers on their timer, programmed to come on
At such a strangely late hour in life
For watering a garden,
Refreshed your sleep four thousand miles away by
Hissing sweetly,
Deepening the smell of green in Eden.
You heard the summer chirr of insects.
You heard a sky of stars.
You didn't know it, fast asleep at dawn in Paris.
You didn't hear a thing.
You heard me calling.
I am no longer human.

France for Boys

There wasn't anyone to thank.
Two hours from Paris in a field.
The car was burning in a ditch.
Of course, the young star of the movie can't be killed off so early.

He felt he had to get off the train when he saw the station
        sign CHARLEVILLE —
Without knowing why — but something had happened there.
Rimbaud explodes with too good,
With the terrible happiness of light.

He was driving fast through
The smell of France, the French trees
Lining the roads with metronomic to stroboscopic
Bringing-on-a-stroke whacks of joyous light.

They were drunk. It had rained.
Going around the Place de la Concorde too fast
On slippery cobbles, and it happened.
Three spill off the motorcycle, two into a paddy wagon.

Eeehaw, Eeehaw, a midsummer night's dream
Down the boulevard along the Seine.
The most beautiful American girl in France
Has just stepped out of a swimming pool, even in a police van.

Eeehaw, Eeehaw,
In a Black Maria taking them to a hospital.
The beautiful apparently thought the donkey she had just met was dying,
And on the spot fell in love.

The wife of the American Ambassador to France
Took her son and his roommate to Sunday lunch
At a three-star restaurant some distance from Paris.
The chauffeur drove for hours to get to the sacred place.

The roommate proudly wore the new white linen suit
His grandmother had given him for his trip to France.
At the restaurant after they ordered he felt sick and left for the loo.
He dropped his trousers and squatted on his heels over the hole.

No one heard him shouting because the loo was in a separate building.
His pal finally came to find him after half an hour.
Since it was Sunday no one could buy him new pants in a store.
No one among the restaurant staff had an extra pair.

White linen summer clouds squatted over Điện Biên Phủ.
It must be 1954 because you soil yourself and give up hope but don't.
The boys are reading *L'Étranger* as summer reading.
My country, 'tis of thee, Albert Camus!

The host sprinted upstairs to grab his fellow Existentialist —
To drag him downstairs to the Embassy's July Fourth garden party.
The Ambassador's son died horribly the following year
In a ski lodge fire.

Eurostar

Japanese schoolgirls in their school uniforms with their school
 chaperones
Ride underwater on a train
Every terrorist in the world would dearly love to bomb
For the publicity and to drown everybody.
The Eurostar dashes into the waves.
The other passengers are watching the Japanese girls eat
Little sweeties they bought with their own money
In London. President Bush the younger is making ice cream.
Ice cream for dessert
Is what Iraq is, without the courses that normally come before.
You eat dessert to start and then you have dessert.
One of them is a Balthus in her short school skirt standing on the seat.
She reaches up too high to get something out of her bag.
She turns around smiling because she knows where you are looking.

CHARLES WRIGHT

Scar Tissue

"At the heart of every poem is a journey of discovery. Something is being found out," Charles Wright has written. In his poems, the same old world we look at every day without seeing it, be it a tree in the yard, the bird in that tree, the branch swaying after the bird has flown, is the subject of endless interest. For Wright, reality is not stable; it changes with the seasons and has to be rediscovered again and again. "I write out my charms and spells / against the passage of light / and gathering evil," he writes in his new book. The mind in the act of finding what will suffice in the face of one's own mortality is Wright's inexhaustible theme. His spiritual and philosophical problem is that he is a "God-fearing agnostic" sure only of his need to question everything. What makes his poems memorable is his seemingly inexhaustible ability to see things with new eyes. In *Scar Tissue*, as in his other books, he is a poet of great originality and beauty.

Appalachian Farewell

Sunset in Appalachia, bituminous bulwark
Against the western skydrop.
An Advent of gold and green, an Easter of ashes.

If night is our last address,
This is the place we moved from,
Backs on fire, our futures hard-edged and sure to arrive.

These are the towns our lives abandoned,
Wind in our faces,
The idea of incident like a box beside us on the Trailways seat.

And where were we headed for?
The country of Narrative, that dark territory
Which spells out our stories in sentences, which gives them an end
                                                and beginning...

Goddess of Bad Roads and Inclement Weather, take down
Our names, remember us in the drip
And thaw of the wintry mix, remember us when the light cools.

Help us never to get above our raising, help us
To hold hard to what was there,
Orebank and Reedy Creek, Surgoinsville down the line.

The Silent Generation II

We've told our story. We told it twice and took our lumps.
You'll find us here, of course, at the end of the last page,
Our signatures scratched in smoke.

Thunderstorms light us and roll on by.
Branches bend in the May wind,
But don't snap, the flowers bend and do snap, the grass gorps.

And then the unaltered grey,
Uncymbaled, undrumrolled, no notes to set the feet to music.
Still, we pull it up to our chins; it becomes our lives.

Garrulous, word-haunted, senescent,
Who knew we had so much to say, or tongue to say it?
The wind, I guess, who's heard it before, and crumples our pages.

And so we keep on, stiff lip, slack lip,
Hoping for words that are not impermanent — small words,
Out of the wind and the weather — that will not belie our names.

The Wrong End of the Rainbow

It must have been Ischia, Forio d'Ischia.
Or Rome. The Pensione Margutta. Or Naples
Somewhere, on some dark side street in 1959

With What's-Her-Name, dear golden-haired What's-Her-Name.
                                        Or Yes-Of-Course
In Florence, in back of S. Maria Novella,
And later wherever the Carabinieri let us lurk.

Milano, with That's-The-One, two streets from the Bar Giamaica.
Venice and Come-On-Back,
                        three flights up,
Canal as black as an onyx, and twice as ground down.

Look, we were young then, and the world would sway to our sway.
We were riverrun, we were hawk's breath.
Heart's lid, we were center's heat at the center of things.

Remember us as we were, amigo,
And not as we are, stretched out at the wrong end of the rainbow,
Our feet in the clouds,
                        our heads in the small, still pulse-pause of age,

Gazing out of some window, still taking it all in,
Our arms around Memory,
Her full lips telling us just those things
                        she thinks we want to hear.

Images from the Kingdom of Things

Sunlight is blowing westward across the unshadowed meadow,
Night, in its shallow puddles,
                                        still liquid and loose in the trees.
The world is a desolate garden,
No distillation of downed grasses,
                        no stopping the clouds, coming at us one by one.

———————

The snow crown on Mt. Henry is still white,
                                        the old smoke watcher's tower
Left-leaning a bit in its odd angle to the world,
Abandoned, unusable.
Down here, in their green time, it's past noon
                        and the lodgepole pines adjust their detonators.

———————

The blanched bones of moonlight scatter across the meadow.
The song of the second creek, with its one note,
                                        plays over and over.
How many word-warriors ever return
                                        from midnight's waste and ruin?
Count out the bones, count out the grains in the yellow dust.

Against the American Grain

Stronger and stronger, the sunlight glues
The afternoon to its objects,
                    the baby pine tree,
The scapular shadow thrown over the pond and meadow grass,
The absence the two
                    horses have left on the bare slope,
The silence that grazes like two shapes where they have been.

The slow vocabulary of sleep
                    spits out its consonants
And drifts in its vowely weather,
Sun-pocked, the afternoon dying among its odors,
The cocaine smell of the wind,
The too-sweet and soft-armed
                    fragrance around the reluctant lilac bush.

Flecked in the underlap, however,
                    half-glimpsed, half-recognized,
Something unordinary persists,
Something unstill, never-sleeping, just possible past reason.
Then unflecked by evening's overflow
                    and its counter current.
What mystery can match its maliciousness, what moan?

North

This is the north, cloud tatters trailing their joints across the ground
And snagging themselves
In the soaked boughs of the evergreens.
Even the heart could lift itself higher than they do,
The soaked and bough-spattered heart,
But doesn't because this is the north,
Where everything dark, desire and its extra inch, holds back
And drags itself, sullen and misty-mouthed, through the trees.
An apparitionless afternoon,
One part water, two parts whatever the light won't give us up.

The north is not the memory of the north but its repeat
And cadences, St. Augustine in blackface, and hand to mouth:
The north is where we go when there's no place left to go.
It's where our altered selves are,
Resplendent and unrepentant and wholly unrecognizable.
We've been here for years,
Fog-rags and rain and sun spurts,
Beforeworlds behind us, slow light spots like Jimmy Durante's fade-out
Hopscotching across the meadow grass.
This is our landscape and our landing zone, this is our dark glass.

Pilgrim's Progress

At the start, it goes like this —
One's childhood has a tremendous shape,
                    and moves like a wild animal
Through the deadfall and understory.
It's endlessly beautiful,
                    elusive and on to something.
It hides out, but never disappears.

Later, the sacred places Delphi and Italy on us,
Flicking and flashing through the forest,
                    half-seen, half-remembered.
And with them the woods itself,
Each tree, each interlude of marsh grass and beaver shade
Something to tug the sleeve with.

In the end, of course, one's a small dog
At night on the front porch,
                    barking into the darkness
At what he can't see, but smells, somehow, and is suspicious of.
Barking, poor thing, and barking,
With no one at home to call him in,
                    with no one to turn the light on.

Little Landscape

To lighten the language up, or to dark it back down
Becomes the blade edge we totter on.
To say what is true and clean,
                              to say what is secret and underground,
To say the things joy can't requite, and to say them well...

This is the first conundrum.
The second is like unto it,
                              the world is a link and a like:
One falls and all falls.
In this last light from midsummer's week,
                              who knows which way to go?

The great blue heron wheels up the meadow
                              and folds into Basin Creek.
Only the fish know which angle his shadow will make.
And what they know is not what he knows,
Which is neither light nor dark nor joy,
                              but is just is, just is.

Time Will Tell

Time was when time was not,
                    and the world an uncut lawn
Ready for sizing. We looked, and took the job in hand.
Birds burst from our fingers, cities appeared, and small towns
In the interim.
                    We loved them all.
In distant countries, tides nibbled our two feet on pebbly shores
With their soft teeth and languorous tongues.
Words formed and flew from our fingers.
                              We listened and loved them all.

Now finitude looms like antimatter, not this and not that,
And everywhere, like a presence one bumps into,
Oblivious, unwittingly,
                    Excuse me, I beg your pardon.
But time has no pardon to beg, and no excuses.

The wind in the meadow grasses,
                              the wind through the rocks,
Bends and breaks whatever it touches.
It's never the same wind in the same spot, but it's still the wind,
And blows in its one direction,
                              northwest to southeast,
An ointment upon the skin, a little saliva,
Time with its murderous gums and pale, windowless throat,
Its mouth pressed to our mouths,
                    pushing the breath in, pulling it out.

The Woodpecker Pecks, but the Hole Does Not Appear

It's hard to imagine how unremembered we all become,
How quickly all that we've done
Is unremembered and unforgiven,
                              how quickly
Bog lilies and yellow clover flashlight our footfalls,
How quickly and finally the landscape subsumes us,
And everything that we are becomes what we are not.

This is not new, the orange finch
And the yellow and dun finch
                              picking the dry clay politely,
The grasses asleep in their green slips
Before the noon can roust them,
The sweet oblivion of the everyday
                              like a warm waistcoat
Over the cold and endless body of memory.

Cloud-scarce Montana morning.
July, with its blue cheeks puffed out like a *putto* on an ancient map,
Huffing the wind down from the northwest corner of things,
Tweets on the evergreen stumps,
                              swallows treading the air,
The ravens hawking from tree to tree, *not you, not you,*
Is all that the world allows, and all one could wish for.

CANADIAN

FINALISTS

KEN BABSTOCK

Airstream Land Yacht

The feature of *Airstream Land Yacht* that seems most
striking, on a first reading, is its range: here we find a
poet who can do almost anything, both formally and in
his exploration of such subject matter as romantic love,
landscape, the body, the city, physical pain, and a joyful
awareness of the sensory details of a world full of marvels
and riddles. Yet no matter what his subject matter is, or
how he chooses to approach it, he never settles for effect:
Ken Babstock can be terse, darkly funny, tender, elegiac,
wise, mysterious, but he is always fresh and always honest.

On a closer acquaintance, however, it is Babstock's
exemplary compassion that dominates this extraordinary
collection. His is a poetry that sees through our errors
and wishful thinking, a poetry that recognizes that "it's
what we think we saw that sticks, never what we see," yet,
in a series of poems of formal and philosophical rigour,
he is able to conclude that "we should be held and for-
given." *Airstream Land Yacht* is a book with a vision, one
in which a reasoned celebration emerges:

> The earth on the roof. Voles over shingles.
> Seven kinds of moss softening the gables.
> And inside, each step a ride
> On the backs of sea birds to a bed on a floor all sky.

Aurora Algonquin

Evidence of a wolf pack's passing marred the otherwise clean
snow basin of the park's Barron Canyon: their in-line
one-two-one's a juddering paragraph of morse —
They'll run a deer down this whitened concourse,

surround and pin it to a cliff face,
or let its own weight send it through thin ice.
I, or the vodka, stood recalling Mr. Marysak explaining
in Geography, rock's rust-red tint as proof of iron-rich

seams when the pinned-up cowl or hood of stars
didn't collapse exactly but popped or blew a stitch;
a familiar seepage in weak-lit jades deepened, altered course

to crimson, and fell in successive tides from directly overhead
till that night entire became a darkroom developing
its notion of a thing outside the visible: pure in deed, and fed.

Windspeed

We were more than a little sullen on the descent —
ticked, really, at the dead-calm state of the air
at the summit of Topsail. Like a row of penitents,
we'd hiked the hard-scrabble straight up, lugging beer

and a designer kite. It was blue and red and meant
to funnel gusts through its windsock frame. Far
from catching a mean updraft, it spent
the afternoon nose down in the crowberries and fir.

What monarch butterfly in Sumatra was so spent,
so drugged or lifeless it couldn't flap one ear-
shaped wing just once and cause a breeze, at least a dent
in the Wedgwood stillness we stood inside up there?

We coiled it and came down. And down on the crescent
of shale, four different kids tugged on the guide wire
of four different kites and hollered and bent
backwards at the strength of their flight. Composure

legged it back to the truck, we lit smokes and began to vent
into our chests. Colin moved first, sidling over near
a glib little pilot and flicking open a Leatherman blade. I went
with it, thumbing the grind-wheel of my Zippo under

the thin string nearest me. It left as if snipped. A parent
saw what his boy had lost and ran over full of hot air,
clutching tongs that pincer-gripped a heat-split wiener.
We shrugged and sniffed as the appendix of string burnt

to a cinder. We were up in the rarer atmosphere,
the social layer, where it often gets hard to breathe, and silent.
A new constellation just then visible over
Belle Isle, specks leaving, signs enacting what signs meant.

The Brave

That's not what we liked. It wasn't for us.
It was pinned to a stream. Ear-marked.
The *arriviste* mashed up with the avant-garde.
We didn't go for that. That wasn't us.

It wasn't quite right. Lacked focus.
Might have tickled the kids, the simple,
Or those others on that other coast,
but not us. It wasn't what we liked.

It was riding a riptide of research
from Pittsburgh. Big deal. Where
was the spit, the spark, the goatish
smell of the real? Who could tell air

from gas, music from dirge, dinghy
from ark amid all that saleable merch?
I'm saying we didn't like it.
And we didn't. How much? Not much.

We couldn't get in. There were no
knobs on its doors. Goes to show
some prefer building walls and floors
to keep us here, outside, looking in.

That's not what we liked and we disliked
when we did with some vigour. Active.
Off the couch and out with the X. Heave
to with No, No, No, and especially Not.

If there were a key here I'd make that 'No'
bigger. Is it clear what wasn't on for us?
It's about cutting out rot. About rigour. About
the men in acumen and the small made

smaller. We didn't like it from the get go.
It was under the sheets as boys, now
it's everywhere and not. Not liking's like
affirming we're here while stretching here

to include whatever isn't. And we're right.
Show me something we didn't like and I'll
show you airtight. Excruciatingly tight.
It wasn't for us and won't be. Ever. Trust me.

The Minds of the Higher Animals

are without exception irresponsible. Which
sounds alarming and is, admittedly, an aberration
(perhaps not funny) of a more valid, thinkable notion,
that dolphins, wolves, chimps, etc., flip a switch

in us, casting klieg light on the frightening solitude
engendered by the very Fifties idea — I know —
that we alone are responsible for our own
consciousness. A friend, who'd taken work as tutor

to a high-school student, leaned over the back wall
of a booth in a pub and told me: of all the thumbnail
sketches he'd done for her, from *Plato* to *Pascal*
and beyond, this Sartrean concept of taking ownership over all

that you know, feel, and do, had proved the most opaque,
the singularly *most inconceivable stupidity*
ever designed to befall a girl, driving her to kick some shitty
desk chair in frustrated disbelief. Now, Reader, make

a face that's meant to express some woeful sense
of pity and surprise, while feeling a cold sickness underneath.
That was my face. I was mumbling things so far from the truth
of what I felt, I could have been a clergy entering the manse,

touching tops of heads, asking how days went, seeking food,
while wishing one or the other end of this circus dead.
The sight of a pint glass didn't cause me to vomit. I didn't
reel, sweating and murderous, out into the street; but my mood

stiffened, grew intractable, opaque; I felt blue flashes inside
that were flares of all the moments I'd sought causality,
a why for each failing of character, somewhere outside
of myself, amounting to a web of reflexive sophistry

that reached back into the years of my life like illness
discovered late, or how rot sets into wood compromising
the strength of a structure by softening its centre. Rising
from my seat, I went and faced a woman whose caress

had eased my passage through some months I couldn't pass
through on my own, she'd been more than kind, I'd
found I couldn't love her at the time, and fled.
So I faced her, and apologized as best I could, given the mass

of people in the pub. 'This is a poem,' she said, 'and that's not
good enough. Around here, we don't let art, no matter
how acutely felt, stand in for what's necessary, true, and right.
Next time you face me, maybe leave you here. End quote.'

Explanatory Gap

It was Nineteen-Eighty-BoreYouToDeath and sex had attached
                                        its lips to Things.
New was no longer the inverse but the utter annihilation
of old. New laws, models, growth on the hedgerows
                            that had to be hacked. New

fear: moles with bleeding edges; monkey bars, merry-go-rounds,
                                        outlawed lawn
darts; the poems of ex-presidents; crack, glue, gas, E; evangelists
on their knees, and a funky steam roiling over from the
                            Unter den Linden.

I hear *Stasi*, I see the *Nordiques*. We can't know what things mean
                                    in the place
where they're meant, or know what's meant by place
with no map in our head. Like those whose hobby

it's become to dog-sled, day-hike, air-lift in to where latitudinal
lines meet the north-south ones at some lonely, never stepped-on
patch of steppe or muskeg mat in Labrador; and they intersect

there, apparently, though there's nothing to see, or nothing
visibly marking the spot other than the spot itself: the mapped
land beneath the numbered globe. Say hello

to coordinates-ordinates-ordnance, and a ground rodent
sniffing the spruce air under a daytime moon.
There'll be a sign here soon.

Expiry Date

Notice those days when everything sounds a little lewd? YIELD
signs at hidden corners, *Downtown Rugs*, the word 'oubliette'

appearing innocently enough in an essay on circus workers, yet
when you've chased it down in the COD it's lying under 'ouananiche'

and looming over 'ouch.' When the eye notes that the pop.
of Ouagadougou sits at 690,000 a shower seems in order.

Should there not be a shield, a form of protection the out-there
can employ against the pushy the blue-lensed

the crotch-clutching urgency making a mess of in-here?
We ought to keep it to ourselves; between ourselves;

draw the curtains. Oughtn't we?...Contractions have begun.
Or when Merrill said to Jackson, *this ought to be fun!*

After all, 'Ouija' comes from french 'oui' and German 'ja.'
It's what we think we saw that sticks, never what we see.

Compatibilist

Awareness was intermittent. It sputtered.
      And some of the time you were seen
         asleep. So trying to appear whole

         you asked of the morning: Is he free
      who is not free from pain? It started to rain
a particulate alloy of flecked grey; the dogs

wanted out into their atlas of smells; to pee
      where before they had peed, and might
         well pee again—though it isn't

         a certainty. What is? In the set,
      called Phi, of all possible physical worlds
resembling this one, in which, at time t,

was written 'Is he free who is not free—'
         and comes the cramp. Do you want
         to be singular, onstage, praised,

         or blamed? I watched a field of sun-
      flowers dial their ruddy faces toward
what they needed and was good. At noon

they were chalices upturned, gilt-edged,
      and I lived in that same light but felt
         alone. I chose to phone my brother,

         over whom I worried, and say so.
      He whispered, lacked affect. He'd lost
my record collection to looming debt. I

forgave him—through weak connections,
      through buzz and oceanic crackle—
         immediately, without choosing to,

         because it was him I hadn't lost; and
      later cried myself to sleep. In that village
near Dijon, called Valley of Peace,

a pond reflected its dragonflies
      over a black surface at night, and
         the nuclear reactor's far-off halo

         of green light changed the night sky
      to the west. A pony brayed, stamping
a hoof on inlaid stone. The river's reeds

lovely, but unswimmable. World death
      on the event horizon; vigils with candles
         in cups. I've mostly replaced my records,

         and acted in ways I can't account for.
      Cannot account for what you're about
to do. We should be held and forgiven.

DON McKAY

Strike/Slip

In *Strike/Slip*, Don McKay walks us out to the uncertain ground between the known and unknown, between the names we have given things and things as they are. This is wonder's territory, and from within it McKay considers a time "before mind or math"; before rock, in human hands, turned over in the mind, becomes stone. The poems confront the strangeness and inadequacy of using language to address the point at which language fails — the point where, "wild and incompetent, / you have no house" — and suggest that in such an unsettled state we might truly pay attention. In McKay's work, attention is the foundation of a poetics and an ethics in which otherness is respected, indeed cherished, for its ability to unhouse. But *Strike/Slip* also speaks to the intimacy of our relationships with time. How, at once metaphysical, practical, and intuitive, the weight of it is thought, felt in the body, and discerned in the landscape as sediment and growth, rust and erosion. McKay's meditations on time's evidence acquire a similar heft, proposing, in their discipline of mind and generosity of spirit, a way to be at home in the world. A book of patience, courage, and quiet eloquence, *Strike/Slip* manifests, like quartz, "Some act of pure attention... simple, naked, perilously perfect."

Loss Creek

He went there to have it
exact. The broken prose of the bush roads.
The piles of half-burnt slash. Stumps
high on the valley wall like sconces
on a medieval ruin. To have it tangible.
To carry it as load rather than as mood
or mist. To heft it — earth measure,
rock measure — and feel its raw drag without phrase
for the voice or handle for the hand.
He went there to hear the rapids curl around
the big basaltic boulders saying
husserl husserl, saying I'll
do the crying for you, licking the schists
into flat skippable discs. That uninhabited laughter
sluicing the methodically shorn valley.
He went there to finger the strike/slip
fissure between rock and stone between Vivaldi's
waterfall and the wavering note a varied thrush
sets on a shelf of air. Recognizing the sweet
perils rushing in the creek crawling
through the rock.
He knew he should not trust such
pauseless syntax.
That he should just say no.
But he went there just the same.

Song of the Saxifrage to the Rock

Who is so heavy with the past as you,
Monsieur Basalt? Not the planet's most muscular
depressive, not the twentieth century.
How many fingerholds
have failed, been blown or washed away, unworthy
of your dignified *avoirdupois*, your strict
hexagonal heart? I have arrived to show you, first
the interrogative mood, then secrets of the niche,
then Italian. Listen, slow one,
let me be your fool, let me sit
on your front porch in my underwear
and tell you risqué stories about death. Together
we will mix our dust and luck and turn ourself
into the archipelago of nooks.

Pond

Eventually water,
having been possessed by every verb —
been rush been drip been
geyser eddy fountain rapid drunk
evaporated frozen pissed
transpired — will fall
into itself and sit.
                              Pond. Things touch
or splash down and it
takes them in — pollen, heron, leaves, larvae, greater
and lesser scaup — nothing declined,
nothing carried briskly off to form
alluvium somewhere else. Pond gazes
into sky religiously but also
gathers in its edge, reflecting cattails, alders,
reed beds and behind them, ranged
like taller children in the grade four photo,
conifers and birch. All of them inverted, carried
deeper into sepia, we might as well say
pondered. For pond is not pool,
whose clarity is edgeless and whose emptiness,
beloved by poets and the moon, permits us
to imagine life without the accident-
prone plumbing of its ecosystems. No,
the pause of pond is gravid and its wealth
a naturally occurring soup. It thickens up
with spawn and algae, while,
on its surface, stirred by every
whim of wind, it translates air as texture —
mottled, moiré, pleated, shirred or
seersuckered in that momentary ecstasy from which
impressionism, like a bridesmaid, steps. When it rains

it winks, then puckers up all over, then,
moving two more inches into metamorphosis,
shudders into pelt.
                          Suppose Narcissus
were to find a nice brown pond
to gaze in: would the course of self-love
run so smooth with that exquisite face
rendered in bruin undertone,
shaken, and floated in the murk
between the deep sky and the ooze?

The Canoe People

Then they set off, they say.
After they had travelled a ways,
a wren sang to one side of them.
They could see that it punctured
a blue hole through the heart
of the one who had passed closest to it, they say.
— Ghandl, "Those Who Stay a Long Way Out to Sea,"
tr. Robert Bringhurst

They're out there, the unformed ones,
shapes in sea mist, half-
coagulated air, in their mossy
second-hand canoe. They're out there, the one
who holds the sky up, and the one who runs on
water, having no names to hang on,
old man's beard to branch, or fasten onto,
kelp to rock, or live in, hermit crab
to whelk shell. Out there,
sticking their soft canoe-nose into every cove
and inlet, the one who holds the bow pole and the
one who always bails, knowing nothing, having no raven side
and eagle side to think with, maundering their wayless way
among the islands, and now even
into English with its one-thing-then-
another-traffic-signalled syntax: out there, never
having heard their keel's bone-crunch on the beach, the terrible
birth cry of the plot, out there, the one who floats
the falcon feather, the one with bulging eyes, and the one
I almost recognize, already victim of the wren's bright
hammered music, bravely wearing in his heart that
delicate blue hole through which, I think,
he listens.

Varves

As I approach the high sandstone cliff with its stacked, individual, terribly numerable varves, I think of George from group, who was unable either to stop collecting newspapers or to throw them out. He would describe — not without some pride, or at least amazement at his own extremity — how his basement, then living room, then bedroom had over the years become filled in with stacks of the *Globe and Mail*, the *Sun*, and the *Glengarry News*, all layered sequentially, until he was reduced to living in middle parts of his hallway and kitchen, his life all but occluded by sedimented public time. Unlike George's collection (which of course I saw only in my mind's eye), the cliff's is open to the eroding elements, so that bits have fallen off to form a talus slope of flat, waferlike platelets at its base. This one in my hand has been clearly imprinted by a leaf — simple, lanceolate, probably an ancestor of our ash or elder. Published but vestigial, gone like an anonymous oriental poet, its image still floating on the coarse grains of summer.

On the flip side, winter. Under the eyelid of the ice. How often I thought of writing you, but the pen hung over the page. All the details on the desk too shy to be inscribed. To settle, to hesitate exquisitely, at last to lie, zero among zeroes. Much listening then, but no audience. Rhetoric elsewhere. Language itself has long since backed out of the room on tiptoe.

Sometimes we believe that we must diagnose the perils of the winter varve, and so do our talk-show hosts and shrinks, who number its shades and phases as though it were pregnancy *renversé*, with suicide at the end instead of a baby. As though death were really death. As though the unspoken were failure. Having misread even the newspapers. Having been deaf to the music of the beech leaves, who will cling to their branches until spring, their copper fading to transparency, making a faint metallic clatter.

Philosopher's Stone

—and when, after I've wasted a lifetime looking,
picking over eskers, browsing beaches, rock shops, slag,
when, after I've up and quit, you suddenly
adopt me, winking from the gravel of the roadside
or the rip-rap of the trail or the
jewels of the rich;
when you renounce your wilderness and move in,
living in my pocket as its sage, as my third,
uncanny testicle, the wise one,
the one who will teach me to desire
only whatever happens;
when you happen in my hand as nothing
supercooled to glass, as the grey
watersmooth rock that slew Goliath or the stone
no one could cast; when you come
inscribed by glaciers, lichened, mossed,
packed with former lives inside you like a dense
mass grave;
              when you cleave,
when you fold,
when you gather sense as *omphalos, inukshut,*
cromlech, when you rift in the stress
of intolerable time;
when you find me as the moon
found Li Po in his drunken boat,
when you speak to my heart of its heaviness, of the soft
facts of erosion, when you whisper in that
tongueless tongue it turns out,
though it can't be,
we both know—

Après Chainsaw

Everything listening at me:
the stumps oozing resin, the birdsong
bouncing off my head like sonar,
the bludgeoned air with its fading
after-echoes. I think of people
herded to a square, staring
at the man on the platform.
Whatever I say now
will be strictly interpreted
and parsed. Is this the way it works,
locking you, stunned, in the imperative,
making a weapon of each tool?
Why can't we just bury innocence instead of
wrecking it over and over, as if
it could never die
enough?
           What I want to say is
somewhere a man steps
softly into a hemlock-and-fir-fringed
pause. Heart full.
Head empty. His lost path
scrawls away behind him. A blue
dragonfly with double wings zags, hovers,
zags. A flicker he can't see
yucks its ghost laugh
into the thin slant light.

Deep Midwinter

Snow had fallen, snow on snow
snow on snow
     — Christina Rossetti

Once upon a time the sky's
eternal silence broke up into bits, fresh
new-angled nothings
sowing the wind with pique.
                              Not wing,
though it flies, nor spirit,
though it isn't and it is, nor song,
though it could be said to sing
inaudibly, and though it falls
it's liable to forget and float
or sift, indulged by gravity, as though
that hard-and-fast rule had gone
soft and slow.
                    Finally
it settles on the earth, eternal
silence once again, but
tangible, depthed, an unbreathed
breath.
             Long ago —
it is always long ago —
before there were beds,
or blankets, or animals to wish
they had them, snow:
                              snow on snow
on snow.

In Aornis

Where each tangle in the foliage
is not a nest, where the wind
is ridden by machines. Aornis,
birdless land, whose uninflected sky extends
like rhetoric to the horizon, *idée
fixe*, tight as Tupperware. Each item
insular, insomniac, attended
by echo and clock. The letters
would rather be numbers, the numbers
disavow Pythagoras. Aornis,
where you don't need mysticism
and you don't need music
to do math. The unsung sun,
it turns out, comes up anyway,
while the rocks and lintels, UV bleached
and birdshit-free, are host
to no Xanthoria. In Aornis,
when it snows, the snow
weighs on the branches and the branches
bend beneath the weight. They know
no junco will descend to instigate
the tiny blizzard like a sneeze
which frees them. Only now and then
one will shrug and shed its load
like an old man who recalls an antique joke
and silently silvers the air.

PRISCILA UPPAL

Ontological Necessities

Who are you? one of Priscila Uppal's poems keeps asking itself. Are you the oyster shell of the new millennium, the sundial waitress in her two-bit automobile with a licence to fish, the wristwatch of the nation, the woman's shelter of the soul? The poems in *Ontological Necessities* are all that and much more. Audacious, irreverent, funny, and, at the same time, deeply serious, they explore our notions of identity and various other conventions we live by, striving to see through the lies. The ever-present horrors of our age, the injustice, the violence, the abuse and slaughter of the innocent, are almost always present. Uppal is a political poet who sounds like no other political poet, someone bound to get into trouble in every political system in the world. Her subject matter tends to be dark, but her telling of it is exhilarating. Every poem in her book comes as a surprise, and that includes the free translation of the Anglo-Saxon poem "The Wanderer" with which the book concludes, and which in her version deals with the Iraq war and the fate of people displaced by such calamities. Uppal has done the rare and difficult thing: she has brought a brand new voice to poetry.

Eighteen

When the monster was eighteen
she gave up smoking. Below the rock garden,
the buried remnants of her addiction

and the suspicion of a little extra stash
to screw the ecosystem. It was good
the shaking had ceased

fine to arrive at the realization of culpability
in the grand scheme of things. Love people,
hate others, leave notes in untidy places,
run over things in cars.

Surely, there was no place for her in this town, and yet,
she owned the pool hall, the hairdresser, the juvenile delinquency centre,
though she was the age of her peers, of her closest friends, of the boys
she'd sucked and fucked out of complacency.

A monster, but when she looked in the mirror,
the glass remained intact, did not crack. She applied
her lipstick one lip at a time. Men with hands
near their crotches didn't give her away
ordering three packs of cigarettes at the jukebox.

They waited for her to turn nineteen.
Then, you understand, they would really have some fun.

Poodle in the Painting

The poodle in the painting is a decoy.
Notice her perfectly curled fur,
her pillbox mane, her dark and beady eyes.

Think that behind the poodle
exists nothing: painting ceases
to derive any sort of meaning without the poodle.

If I told you that the poodle was not in fact a poodle
but only resembled a poodle because you cannot
fully picture death, would you believe me, or would
you find this whole adventure déclassé?

Never shot a poodle; but I will shoot
the poodle in this painting. We've not much
to say to each other and the night is very long.

Ontological Necessity

I'd like to bruise this earth
with mental missives until it cracks. If a volcano's brain
contains each eruption, we too must have these splits,
these dungeon pits inside us.

The harvest is nuclear.
My mouth, an octagon; my chest, an FBI file.
Stem cells grow off my neighbour's balcony, fall into my tea.
Cancer paid my tuition. On and on the hurricane
spies and trades. No one watches television
for the stories. Our universe is fresh out of those.
The galaxy yawns and pops pills.

Dear Self,
How am I to know if You are still alive?

Test me, you reply.

Elegy for a Deadbeat Dad

Don't come around here no more. Write that
on my tombstone. Keep your flowers. They give
me the willies, and I've got too many shakes
as it is. Recite a limerick, not a prayer.
It's a joke here. Give your old man
the luxury of a joke now and then. I never
put much faith in ceremony.

Remember when your mother took the hamper of money?
You don't. I guess that was before your time. She had a sense of humour,
then, that woman was wild, believe it or not. She clipped each crisp bill
to the clothesline until they flew away. I called them fighter pigeons, after,
of course, after I calmed down. Your mother said once you were old
                                                                  enough
to understand, you too wouldn't want no dirty business in the house.
                                                                  She still
let me touch her once or twice after that, but the writing was on the wall
and it spoke like my own mother, and I had no need for two.
I hope we can agree that no one needs two.

And as for fathers, I guess no one needs two of those either. Stepkids.
You heard about them I bet. They're ok, I guess. Probably'll stop by
with cheese and crackers or a pie or something. I wish I could be buried in
a cigar box. Tell the minister that's my wish. That kind of thing.

The freaky thing about living is that it goes on while you're busy trying
                                                                  to beat it.
I had a perfect cribbage hand once, framed and hung it in the kitchen.
No one ever dared move it, but I guess some asshole at the Sally Ann
is going to drive away with it in his back seat for a buck or two.
I wanted to give it to you.

This is no time, I suppose, to dwell on what we can't do.
I hear you're a good kid. You shacked up with some nice woman.
Hope it works out. You should have a couple of kids, too,
just to see what it's about.

Now, take your old man down to the corner. I'm tired and hungry,
and this town's got no clock and no women
to distract us.

Let's get polluted.
Whadda ya say?

No Angels in This Death Poem

Absolutely no angels in this death poem.
Half-baked poets offer angels for consolation
the way neighbours offer fruitcake at Christmas.

Absolutely no talk of Christmas in this death poem.
Resurrection went out with yesterday's trash and
holy stars and wise men appear on hockey jerseys.

Absolutely no wise men in this death poem.
Wise men have never made dying understandable.
They've drawn no pie charts or graphs for the soul.

Absolutely no mention of souls in this death poem.
The soul is not a ship, or a bird, or a flag, or a flower.
We have no power of attorney over it, no death connection.

Absolutely no mention of death in this death poem.
Angels are listening and the wise men are sketching.
Look at where all these souls are headed and tell no one.

On the Psychology of Crying Over Spilt Milk

According to Freud's observations and analysis of his nephew fantasy-making with a shoe, the *fort-da* game is the necessary foundational basis by which a child can rightfully count on a parent who leaves for work or an office party or a trip to the Bahamas with her younger lover to eventually return.

The child, controlling the outcome, sees that through simple will and aggression he can force the shoe to go, then facilitate retrieval whenever he so desires. This, according to Freud, makes it easier for the child to accept separation of all kinds. *Fort-da* is *mourning play.*

Hence, in tragedies, shoes play important roles. Actors must think carefully about where to step. Frequently, prints are drawn in light chalk on the stage. No one likes to share a pair. Letters are pulled from their lips, as are knives. When boots find their mark, victims claim the soles.

Children must be encouraged to play *fort-da.* Freud said so, and he had very healthy relationships. For those of you whose parents have left and never returned, you happen to be screwed, psychologically speaking. Perhaps, as in the most successful tragedies, you should seek revenge.

Her Organs Were Drying Up

Over the years father told me that several men in white suits
brought babies to my mother. He used the term *swaddled*
and so I took his word for it.

The white suits gleamed in the moonlight, which father
insisted was providence. I've never understood
providence although I've looked it up
on at least five different occasions.

My mother was on her knees in the garden
sucking on blueberries, but father felt
it wise to leave out such unimportant details.
An apple or *a peach* and what would have been different?

I opened my mouth and *Good God!* came out.
My father was worried I'd end up religious.
My mother was merely worried.

Several men in white suits stood in the shadows
with buckets and buckets of water and children trapped
in flowerpots singing *We are the glory of the earth.*

Father's Wheelchair Is Purchased by the Smithsonian

The tall men weren't necessary. We all said so.
Nominated by the triumvirate keepers of historical destiny,
my father acquiesced the artifact with little fuss.

When they hoisted him up, he made only a slight whimper,
the kind of noise that should be blamed upon reflex
rather than resistance, and his eyeglasses fell to the floor

from the force of gravity. My father is cooperative.
All his papers are in order, and he would have been happy to donate
his chair to the authorities, no deal was necessary.

Not that we destroyed the documents, on the contrary, we kept them.
My father's sheets are stuffed with duplicates. Without the vehicle
and since our arms are easily exhausted, he spends

much more time in bed than he used to, but old habits die hard.
Every spoon needs a fork! Every sun needs a moon!
Poor wheelchair, he cries, *you're empty without me!*

It is truly debatable what you *should* or *should not* have taken
that day. The deal we struck was for the wheelchair
and the wheelchair only (as the object which most represented

my father in his time). Every day, other things go missing.
First his shirts, then socks, then teeth. I can't wait
for the exhibit to open (they keep promising *soon soon*)

so all of us who love him can climb up on his chair again.
So my brother can go back to patrolling the neighbourhood.
So my mother can resume that nasty business of having children.

Common Book Pillow Book

Long enough since the genre was popular
we've forgotten what to call it: weird mix of quotes and collectibles, private
thoughts and uncensored meditations in brief, like locks of hair and
child height charts of your considerations
and ponderings. An abandoned art, you practise it with care: each quote
equal to the other, simple entries like coordinates of unmarked

appearances

in the sky — twenty years, over
8,000 days — the weather is "what you make of sunshine," and only

women "can

make a man successful," haven't you heard
"God is the messenger, and we are all brothers and sisters," organizations
of hate "must be fought with the ultimate crest: humanity," and you
note a quote with a love reserved
for precision and the unattained, and I
suspend like cracked meteors in the ether
of your common message: go to bed, what is truly important in this world
has already been said.

"When people deserve love the least
is when they need it the most," we are the axis
of cliché, "like mother like daughter," sign your name
on this one before I turn out the light
and resume my interrupted prayer.

ABOUT THE POETS

KEN BABSTOCK is the author of *Mean* (1999), which won the Atlantic Poetry Prize and the Milton Acorn People's Poet Award, and *Days Into Flatspin* (2001), winner of a K. M. Hunter Award. His poems have won Gold at the National Magazine Awards, have been anthologized in Canada and the United States, and have been translated into Dutch, Serbo-Croatian, and Latvian. Ken Babstock lives in Toronto.

PAUL FARLEY won the Arvon Poetry Competition in 1996. His first poetry collection, *The Boy from the Chemist Is Here to See You* (1998), won the Forward Poetry Prize for Best First Collection and a Somerset Maugham Award and was shortlisted for the Whitbread Poetry Award. He was named the *Sunday Times* Young Writer of the Year in 1999. He received an Arts Council Writers' Award in 2000. *The Ice Age* (2002) won the Whitbread Poetry Award and was shortlisted for the T. S. Eliot Prize. In addition to being shortlisted for the Griffin Poetry Prize, Paul Farley's *Tramp in Flames* won the Forward Prize for Best Individual Poem for "Liverpool Disappears for a Billionth of a Second." He lives in Lancashire, where he lectures in Creative Writing at the University of Lancaster.

RODNEY JONES is the author of eight books of poetry, including *The Story They Told Us of Light* (1980), *The Unborn* (1985), *Transparent Gestures* (1989), *Apocalyptic Narrative and Other Poems* (1993), *Things That Happen Once* (1996), *Elegy for the Southern Drawl* (1999), and *Kingdom of the Instant* (2002). He was a finalist for the Pulitzer Prize and the winner of the 1989 National Book Critics Circle Award. His other honours include a Guggenheim Fellowship, the Peter I. B. Lavan Award from the Academy of American Poets, the Jean Stein Award from the American Academy and Institute of Arts and Letters, a Southeast Booksellers Association Award, and a Harper Lee Award. Rodney Jones is a professor of English at Southern Illinois University at Carbondale.

DON MCKAY has published ten previous works of poetry. He is the winner of two Governor General's Literary Awards for Poetry, for *Night Field* (1991) and for *Another Gravity* (2000). He has been shortlisted twice for the Griffin Poetry Prize, first in 2001 for *Another Gravity* and more recently in 2005 for *Camber: Selected Poems* (2004), which was also named a *Globe and Mail* Notable Book of the Year. Don McKay lives in British Columbia.

FREDERICK SEIDEL's previous collections include *Final Solutions: Poems, 1959–1979*; *Sunrise* (1980), which won the National Book Critics Circle Award in Poetry and the Lamont Prize; *My Tokyo* (1993); *Going Fast* (1998); *The Cosmos Poems*, illustrated by Anselm Kiefer (2000); *Life on Earth* (2001); and *Area Code 212* (2002). Frederick Seidel is the recipient of numerous prizes, including the 2002 PEN/Voelker Award for Poetry. He is a founding editor of *The Paris Review*, a protégé of Ezra Pound and Robert Lowell, and one of the original Elaine's crowd. He lives in New York City.

PRISCILA UPPAL is the author of four previous collections of poetry, *How to Draw Blood from a Stone* (1998), *Confessions of a Fertility Expert* (1999), *Pretending to Die* (2001), and *Live Coverage* (2003), and the novel *The Divine Economy of Salvation* (2002), which was published by Doubleday in Canada and by Algonquin Books of Chapel Hall in the United States and has been translated into Dutch and Greek. Her poetry has been translated into Korean, Croatian, Latvian, and Italian. Priscila Uppal lives in Toronto and is a professor of Humanities at York University and coordinator of York's Creative Writing Program.

CHARLES WRIGHT's books of poetry include *The Grave of the Right Hand* (1970); *Hard Freight* (1973); *Bloodlines* (1975); *China Trace* (1977); *The Southern Cross* (1981); *The Other Side of the River* (1984); *Zone Journals* (1988); *The World of the Ten Thousand Things: Poems 1980–1990* (1990); *Chickamauga* (1995), which won the Academy of American Poets' Lenore Marshall Poetry Prize; *Black Zodiac* (1997), which received the Pulitzer Prize for Poetry; *Appalachia* (1998); *Negative Blue: Selected Later Poems* (2000); *A Short History of the Shadow* (2002); and *Buffalo Yoga* (2004). He has received a Guggenheim Fellowship, the National Book Award in Poetry, and the PEN Translation Prize. Charles Wright is a professor of English at the University of Virginia at Charlottesville, where he lives.

ACKNOWLEDGEMENTS

The publisher thanks the following for their kind permission to reprint the work contained in this volume:

"The Lapse," "Liverpool Disappears for a Billionth of a Second," "The Newsagent," "Brutalist," "Tramp in Flames," "An Ovaltine Tin in the Egg Collections at Tring," "'A Shepherd's Guide to Wool and Earmarks,'" "The Scarecrow Wears a Wire," "Paperboy and Air Rifle," and "The Westbourne at Sloane Square" from *Tramp in Flames* by Paul Farley are reprinted by permission of Picador, an imprint of Pan Macmillan Ltd.

"I Find Joy in the Cemetery Trees," "The Work of Poets," "TV," "The Assault on the Fields," and "Sitting with Others" from *Salvation Blues: One Hundred Poems, 1985–2005* by Rodney Jones are reprinted by permission of Houghton Mifflin Company.

"From Nijinsky's Diary," "On Being Debonair," "Homage to Pessoa," "Fog," "The Owl You Heard," "France for Boys," and "Eurostar" from *Ooga-Booga* by Frederick Seidel are reprinted by permission of Farrar, Straus and Giroux.

"Appalachian Farewell," "The Silent Generation II," "The Wrong End of the Rainbow," "Images from the Kingdom of Things," "Against the American Grain," "North," "Pilgrim's Progress," "Little Landscape," "Time Will Tell," and "The Woodpecker Pecks, but the Hole Does Not Appear" from *Scar Tissue* by Charles Wright are reprinted by permission of Farrar, Straus and Giroux.

"Loss Creek," "Song of the Saxifrage to the Rock," "Pond," "The Canoe People," "Varves," "Philosopher's Stone," "Après Chainsaw," "Deep Midwinter," and "In Aornis" from *Strike/Slip* by Don McKay are reprinted by permission of McClelland & Stewart Ltd.

"Eighteen," "Poodle in the Painting," "Ontological Necessity," "Elegy for a Deadbeat Dad," "No Angels in This Death Poem," "On the Psychology of Crying Over Spilt Milk," "Her Organs Were Drying Up," "Father's Wheelchair Is Purchased by the Smithsonian," and "Common Book Pillow Book" from *Ontological Necessities* by Priscila Uppal are reprinted by permission of Exile Editions Ltd.